Passion for *Pattern*

First published in Great Britain 2007 by Unipress Cumbria
First edition of 2000 softbound copies
Copyright © 2007 photography: Richard Archer, Tim Hill,
Zoë Hill, Raymond Honeyman, Roger Lee, Debbie Patterson
and Rosemary Weller
Copyright © text: named authors

Photograph of Mary Schoeser courtesy BBC Homes and
Antiques Magazine

With special thanks to Ehrman Tapestry, Liberty of London
and Viyella

Every endeavour has been made to obtain copyright permission
to reproduce all the images in this book.

British Library cataloguing in publication data
Date for this publication is available from the British Library

ISBN: 978 1 869979 23 2

Designed by Claire Andrews
Published with the support of the University of Cumbria
Printed by Reeds Printers, Penrith, Cumbria

Printed on Hello Silk which is certified to the ISO14001
environmental management standard

A Passion for Painting Pattern

The textile designs of
Raymond Honeyman

Foreword by
Mary Schoeser

Unipress Cumbria

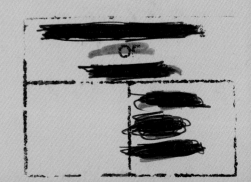

To Richard from Raymond with love

10th August 2007

Raymond Honeyman occupies an anachronistic position, being perfectly in tune with the demands and possibilities of present-day textile print production, and yet consciously electing to express his design ideas in a manner that would be considered by many to be 'quaint'. His medium is gouache, painstakingly applied to capture on paper what is – in his current series of work – essentially a trompe l'oeil rendition of a printed canvas. These pieces have been commissioned by Ehrman Tapestries, to whose collections he has contributed since 1997. For Hugh Ehrman, what Honeyman brings to this prestigious range of needlepoint kits (which is renowned for its designs by Kaffe Fassett among others) is a "fantastic sense of pattern and tremendously rich sense of colour". Of the artist's means of working Ehrman stresses that "the meticulous detail gives an extra dimension: the craft skill is what puts it on a higher level . . . "[1]

The needlepoint designs represent Honeyman's latest approach to designing for textiles in a career that since 1976 has encompassed a breadth of work, all of which expresses his continuing preoccupation with pattern. His first sale was to Susan Collier, purchasing on behalf of Liberty of London. As a creator of fashion and furnishing fabrics, his designs have entered the ranges of numerous companies based in the UK and New York, as well as Austrian, German, Japanese, Portuguese and Swiss firms. Often these went via the Keith Robson Studio, Nottingham, with whom Honeyman was associated – sometimes part-time, sometimes full-time – from 1986 until 1997. Robson knew Honeyman's work from the period when he employed the latter at Viyella. There, as a member of the studio from 1979-1982 (and as print producer from 1980), Honeyman quickly made the transition from painting in watercolour to painting in gouache. Robson preferred this medium for practical reasons: Viyella was difficult to print and, to minimize risk, designs needed to show no variation within each individual area of colour. More than this, however, he recalls that

Raymond's design work also suited gouache, as did his particular colour skill and handling of pattern: "Viyella had a long tradition of classical motifs and Raymond's interpretation was 'Arts and Craftsy' but modern – his is a unique style in that it keeps the historical feel but with a very forward look". [2]

Robson might well be describing a much more recent group of Honeyman's stylized floral needlepoint designs for Ehrman, which do more than achieve an updating of the William Morris style. Instead, these designs from the 2000/1 and 2002/3 collections, with simple descriptive titles such as 'Thistle', 'Bluebell' and 'Lily of the Valley', accord with what Dr Jennifer Harris has identified as a key component of art textiles, which not only "use textiles for their tactile and symbolic qualities but also to 'initiate debate about textile history' ".[3] Honeyman's engagement with this debate stems from his vivid recollections of a shop in his home town of Perth, in which hung a length of 1960's revived William Morris fabric. He describes its mesmerizing effect, and in 'Thistle' and his other works, one sees how complete was his absorption of the design theory by which its pattern was constructed. There is a less singular explanation for his facility with the Persian/Indian approach to pattern as characterised by designs such as 'Punjabi Paisley' (1997), 'Indian Garden' (1998/99) and his 2006/7 limited edition design, 'Paisley Splendour', although, to a native Scot, the Paisley pattern stands as much as a record of textile heritage as does the tartan. Of the latter, Honeyman's playful intervention with this sometimes sombre plaid – seen in 'Tartan Fan' (2005/6) – questions the straightforward and manly associations of this pattern (for even Vivienne Westwood's use of tartan retained the warrior-like implications) by its juxtaposition to a shape that is redolent of the coy and the flirtatious.

The fan shape itself, a Honeyman innovation within the Ehrman oeuvre, appeared first in 'Daisy Fan' (1998/99). While its stems, variously coloured to suggest 'pulsating' leaves, bring to mind the neon lights of an Art Deco cinema, in truth its rhythmic sensibilities owe far more to the artist's other talents. His finesse at the piano and on the dance floor – inherited from his mother and father respectively – draw upon an aural and spatial comprehension of pattern that accounts for his ability to improvise with gouache. This is not at first apparent when looking at a completed work, but as carefully constructed as his finished designs appear, they are not pre-sketched or belaboured in their geometry. Instead they begin with an idea and grow spontaneously as he paints, often exploring the freedom that needlepoint canvas allows, by repeating a shape but never the colouration, as in 'Paper Fans' (2003/4). From the same collection is 'Mikado Maids', a tour de force of contrapuntal exchanges and juxtapositions of pattern and colour that has, not surprisingly, become a best-seller for Ehrman. This fact squares with several trends: the growth of interest in needlepoint itself [4], the desire among stitchers for something more demanding [5], and the less textile-specific drive towards the 'massclusive'. For the latter, Emma Crichton-Miller explains, "Minimalism has had its day; softer values like narrative, local tradition and individuality are back in play – they're what 'massclusive' means. As Professor Tom Barket, who led the IDE project puts it, 'Mass production has been explored to its limits. It's as good as it gets. This renaissance of artisan values is driven by hard commercial logic.' It's as if we'd suddenly re-embraced William Morris." [6]

In a debate that has come to characterize the visual arts in the early years of the third millennium, the role of skill, or craft as it is often called, has been returned to the top of many an agenda, brought there by interconnected developments – in the UK, in art education for example, by the increase in student enrolment as well as in computer-aided design systems. These parallel growths have changed concepts of individuality as much as the manner in which many designs are created. Honeyman has witnessed these changes first hand, both as a designer and as a print producer. Aside from his experience of this latter position

at Viyella, he also oversaw production in the UK, the USA and Europe from 1991-93 for Collier Campbell Limited, and recently took the same role on an informal basis for 'Venezia' and 'Parisian Stripe', the digitally-printed scarves he designed for Ehrman in 2007. Yet Honeyman, with twenty five years' experience as a lecturer and eleven as an examiner, insists on the primacy of drawing even more so today. Indeed, in his view, "If you can't draw, you can't see . . . "[7] Here again, he is in good company: on the development of leading-edge computer graphics, Dr Jane Harris has recently commented on "computer graphics conferences where there have been teams of researchers, say 50 people with EU money, millions and millions to make cloth 'work' better". Asking what she's invented in software terms, her response is that they "should just all go and do textile degrees. They can't make it look the same way we do because they don't have the material knowledge, and I mean hands on".[8]

Within this context, Honeyman's artwork makes essential viewing. It challenges the assumption that pattern-making is passé, and this is not at all unconscious. He knows he stands apart from the world of the digital, with its oft-belied promise of the quick, slick fix. Instead, his work demonstrates an unequivocal passion for pattern, and even more so, for pattern that is painted. That the hands on is essential to Honeyman is indicated by his decision, in 1995, to leave a full-time teaching position at the Scottish College of Textiles for his present part-time position at the University of Cumbria, to allow more time to satisfy his need to paint. This has long been the case. Even as a Diploma student at Duncan of Jordanstone College of Art in Dundee, he preferred to paint, rather than print, his designs. As a result, and notwithstanding his receipt of the highest degree – a Highly Commended – it was only with the support of his external examiners, Audrey Levy and Peter Simpson, that he was allowed to go on for a year of postgraduate studies. He is quick to express his gratitude for such foresighted support, as indeed for the opportunity, on graduating in 1976, to be the sole representative of the college at 'Texprint 1', at the Design Centre, London. As a result receiving coverage in *Design* magazine, he also sold his first design, to Liberty of London, and with other sales established his reputation with firms such as Viyella.

Undoubtedly, his skill as a painter (and he nearly pursued this course instead of Decorative Design at Dundee) is what garnered such attention, but his approach has not always since then been in favour, especially as methodologically-driven, concept-laden work became sought within academic circles. Even today the subtle painted references to other textile forms, whether in the Bouquet pair (2000/1), evoking net curtains at farmhouse windows in interwar France, or Greek Ribbons (2005/6), deceptively simple yet with 19 colours, might easily escape the jaded viewer, in search of ever more blatant paradigms. However, as craft itself now emerges as a force within contemporary art, so present-day critics note of painting that "while of course it never disappeared as an art it [had] moments when it seemed simply old-fashioned, with nowhere to go. Well, today it is back in intellectual favour with a vengeance."[9] This leaves room, once more, for Honeyman's work to be appreciated, straddling as it does the commercial and the unique, the personification and the personal. In a 2000 *Stitcher's World* feature on his Ehrman commissions – aside from stating that his "dramatic canvases . . . are some of the most exquisitely beautiful in needlepoint today" – the journalist, Michelle Howard, also rather presciently added, "And Raymond Honeyman is just getting started".[10] That he is, is in no small measure due to his passion for painting pattern, for with it he proves that skill is essential; without it, artistry is gone.

Mary Schoeser

1. Interview with Hugh Ehrman, 28 March 2007.
2. Interview with Keith Robson, 28 March 2007.
3. Jessica Hemmings, 'Sign Post to a New Space', *Fiberarts*, Apr/May 2006, p.8.
4. "As the recent knitting craze is dying down, needlepoint continues its steady growth." Gretchen Wahl, 'On point: new stitch trend...' *Crain's Chicago Business* 12/12/2005 at www.highbeam.com
5. "I do find that the sophistication of the designs...make the stitcher join the designer in their journey. I could not see myself working on some of the simplistic and twee designs available in the high street." Tony Wilson-Ing, Lieutenant Colonel retired, *Ehrman Tapestry 2005-6*, p.33. 6. Emma Crichton-Miller, 'Found in Translation', *Crafts* 203 Nov/Dec 2006, p.22. The IDE project is the Royal College of Art's Industrial Design and Engineering faculty's 'Go Global' scheme, which takes students into a non-western country to collaborate with local designers.
7. Interview with Raymond Honeyman, 19 March 2007.
8. Nick Barley, 'Jane Harris and Timorous Beasties in Conversation', *Crafts* 205 Mar/Apr 2007, p.32.
9. Marina Vaizey, 'By Hand: the use of craft in contemporary art', *Crafts* 204 Jan/Feb 2007, p.64.
10. Michelle Howard, 'Symphony of Sight: exploring the lavish works of Scotland's Raymond Honeyman', *Stitcher's World* Feb/Mar 2000, p.20.

"The process of drawing and painting is an intimate experience of serene tranquility."

Home and Family

The beautiful city of Perth, Scotland where I was born and brought up.

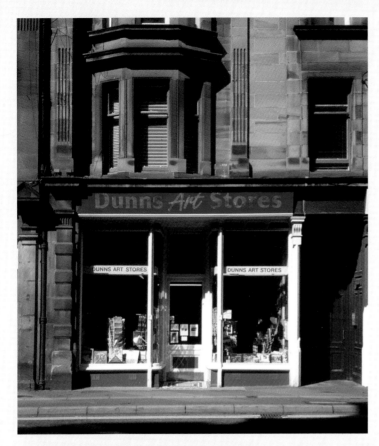

When I was a young boy my favourite shop was always Dunns Art Stores where I would go and browse for hours amidst the shelves of pencils, papers and paint tubes. If asked what I would like for my birthday or Christmas I almost always would ask for paints and paper.

After Sunday School on Sunday afternoons my gran sometimes would take my brother Kenneth and me to Perth Museum and Art Gallery which I loved. I still love it and always visit the gallery when in Perth.

My grandfather, Thomas Honeyman, owner of Honeyman's Stores.

My mother, Edna Honeyman taken in the 1940s.

My father, Peter Honeyman (on the right of the picture with the two-tasseled sporran).

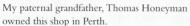

My paternal grandfather, Thomas Honeyman owned this shop in Perth.

My maternal grandfather, Edward Smith owned this Temperance Bar in Dundee where my brother and I would be taken to sip sasparilla and cream sodas.

"I delight in being able to create and combine pattern with pattern."

Inspiration

My inspiration can come from many sources, but I am undoubtedly attracted to the old rather than the new. I can find exquisite beauty in faded colours, tattered edges and threadbare surfaces and can be enthralled by the beguiling charm of an untouched interior from a bygone era. I am an avid gatherer of old and aged artefacts and instinctively surround myself with ever-changing assemblages of colourful, decorative objects which uplift my spirits. These photographs show some of my personal collections.

My collections of old
fans and parasols.

My wardrobe heavily laden with old cases, boxes and hats.

My collection of old tartan
music books and boxes.

My treasured collection of
tartan ties . . . all second hand.

Some old flags and
royal memorabilia.

"Colour is unquestionably the most important aspect of designing textiles as our instinctive response to seeing colour stirs our emotions."

Greece

Painted artwork for 'Greek Ribbons'
I designed this wanting to celebrate fond
memories I have of many trips to Greece.

Me buying some old Greek textiles in Galerie
Varsakis on the island of Skiathos. This is one
of my favourite shops. The enchanting interior
lifts my spirits as it is always brimming with an
abundance of beautiful old Greek artefacts.

"My ideas usually emerge from an emotional reaction to an exhilarating visual experience such as the glory of a summer garden, a lavish, theatrical stage performance or the faded splendour of an old Parisian café."

Liberty of London

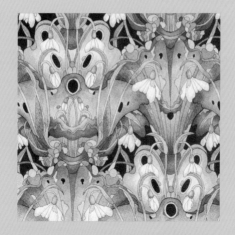

"Drawing helps one to see."

After graduating from Duncan of Jordanstone College of Art in
Dundee I travelled to London to show my portfolio of designs.
The first design I ever sold was 'Snowdrops' which was bought by
Susan Collier for Liberty of London. I was thrilled. Liberty bought
a few more of my designs over the years but the excitement of this
first sale was memorable.

Susan Collier was then print producer for Liberty, but
later, with her sister Sarah Campbell formed the renowned and
celebrated company Collier Campbell, for whom I have had the
privilege to work from time to time.

"The intense joy of choosing and placing colours together resonates with my soul."

Greeting Cards and Wrapping Papers

'Snowdrops'

'Morning Glory'

'Daffodils'

Two of my designs were featured in Design magazine a few months after I graduated from art college. The company Philyum Ridd in Cambridge saw them and consequently commissioned me to design a set of floral wrapping papers and greeting cards.

'Roses'

"I have always found the continual, never-ending movement of intricate repeating pattern mesmerizing."

Viyella

Viyella is a distinctive fabric with an illustrious history, and is woven with a special yarn spun from a unique blend of wool and cotton.

Kashan Collection

The 'Kashan' collection was designed for Viyella and was inspired by the opulence of ancient Persian carpets.

Painted artwork for 'Persian Stripe'

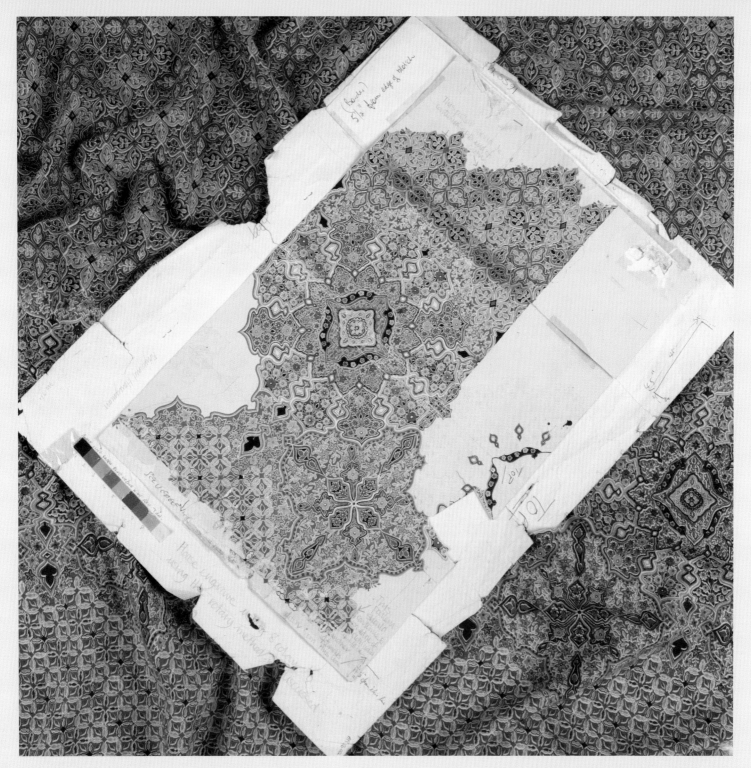

Painted artwork for 'Persian Border'

Painted artwork for 'Persian Blossom'

40

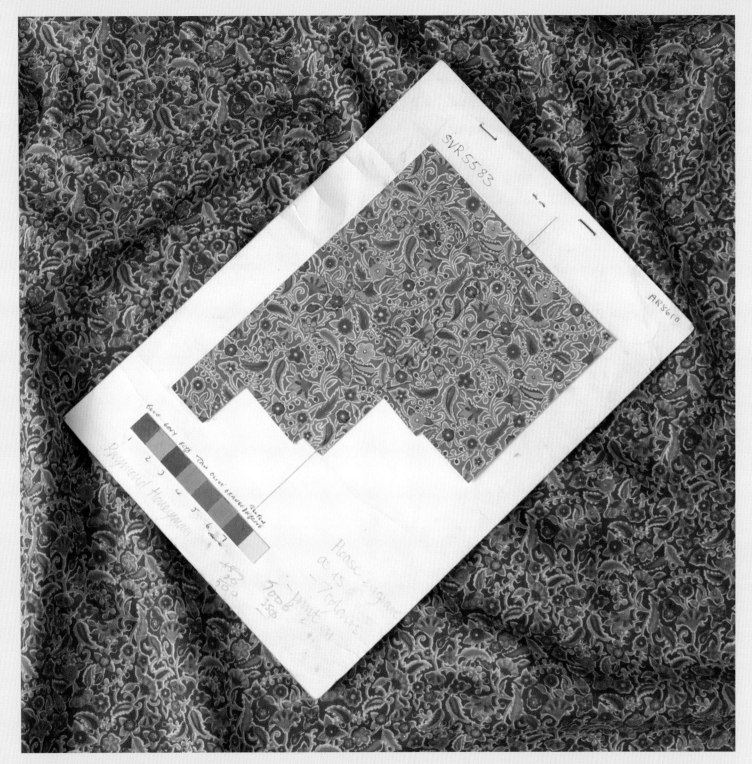

Painted artwork for 'Persian Fern'

41

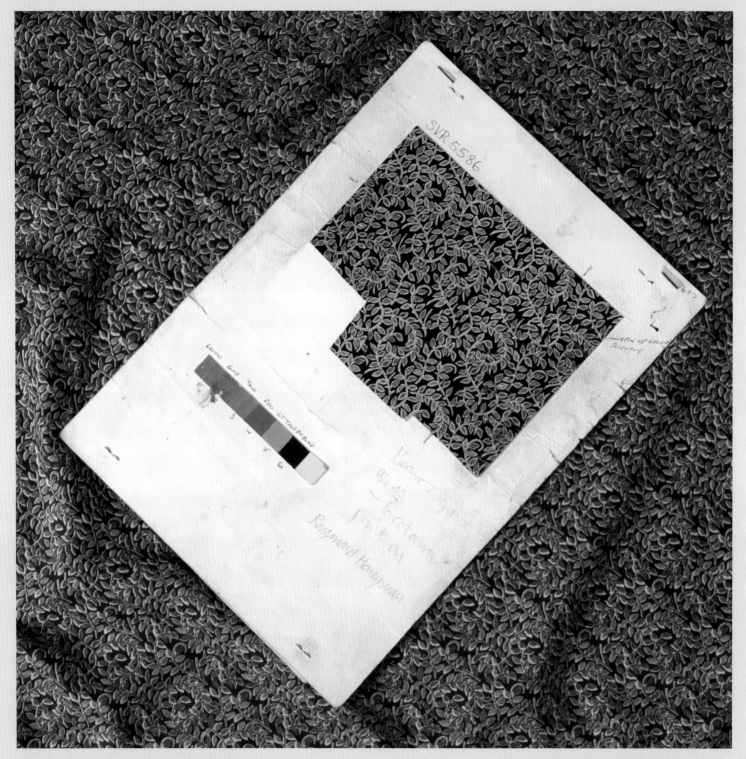

Painted artwork for 'Persian Leaf'

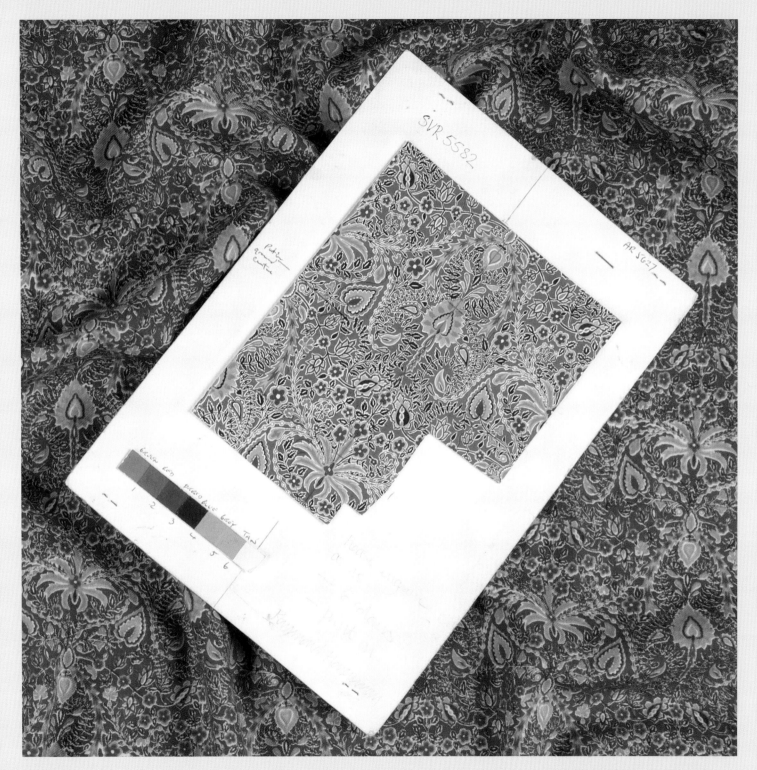

Painted artwork for 'Persian Garden'

43

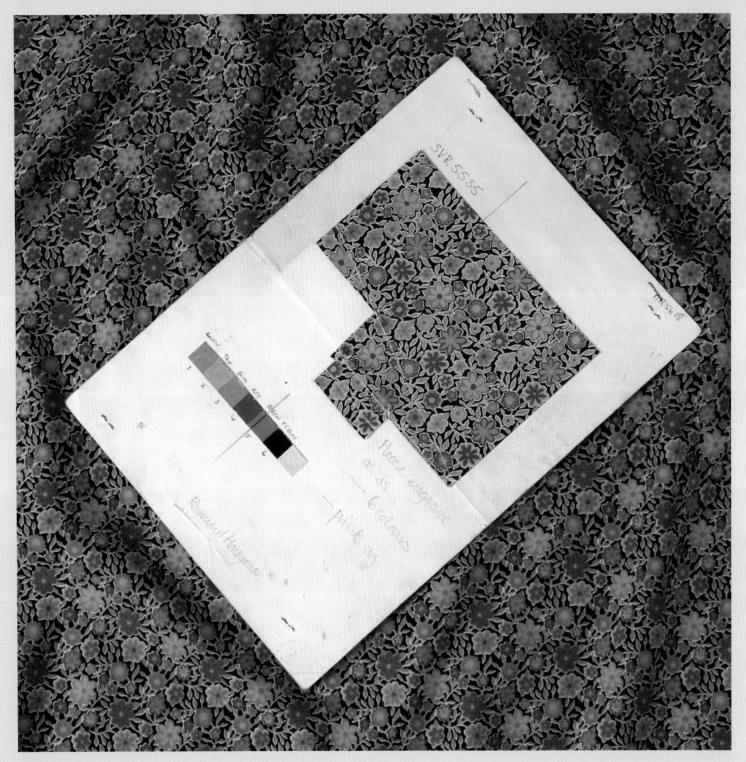

Painted artwork for 'Persian Flower'

Chinoiserie Collection

The 'Chinoiserie' collection was designed for Viyella and was inspired by antique Chinese costume.

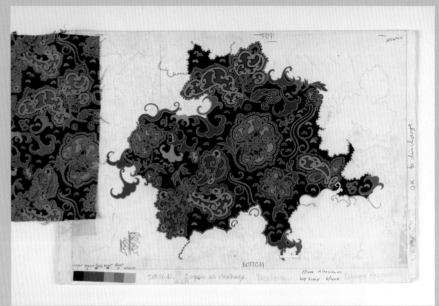

Painted artwork for 'Peking Peony'

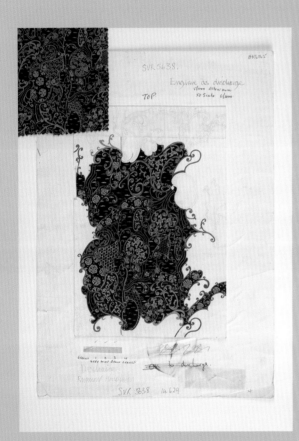

Painted artwork for 'Shanghai Mosaic'

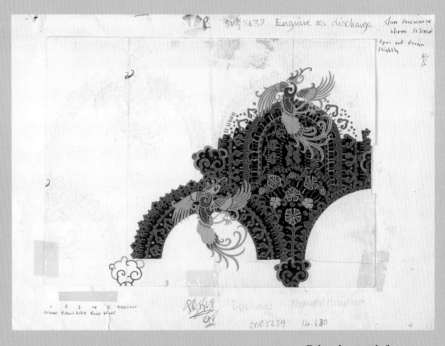

Painted artwork for 'Shanghai Birds'

Painted artwork for
'Peking Flowers'

> "Painting is a sensual activity...
> I love the feel of the brush in the
> paint pot and the sensation of
> paint–laden bristles leaving colour
> on the paper."

For years I admired the Ehrman Tapestry collections. Although I had been designing printed textiles, one day I decided to telephone Ehrman. I spoke directly to Hugh Ehrman and explained that I would love to design some tapestries. I sent some photographs of my print designs and he called me to say that he liked them very much, and asked me to go to London to meet him and show him my artwork. He commissioned me to do one design, which was 'Magic Carpet' and I am delighted to say that he has commissioned me to design for the Ehrman Tapestry collections ever since.

I usually spend several weeks painting out each tapestry design which is a personal and sublimely entrancing process. I begin by sketching ideas to visualise the imagery and possible compositions. I then draw out my design with a very sharp pencil so that I can place every single detail where I want it to be. Most of my designs have 144 stitches per square inch and I paint out each and every one of them. I always aim to make every square inch glow with an effusion of sumptuous colour. Choosing the colours is always an exhilarating pleasure. When I begin to paint a design I almost become attached to it. I carry my drawing board around the house and place it so that I can study and contemplate what I have done whilst having lunch. I often take the design to my bedroom so that I can lie in bed and ponder the next stage in the hushed late hours of the night.

Ehrman

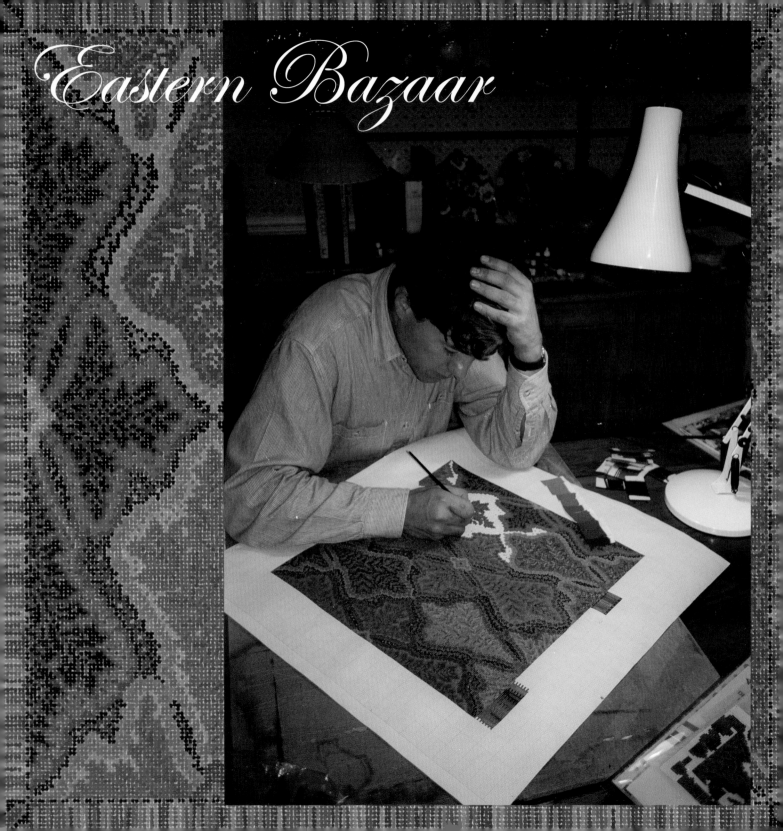

Eastern Bazaar

Painted artwork for 'Magic Carpet'
This was my first design for Ehrman Tapestry. I found some old
sepia photographs of old Eastern Bazaars showing lavish displays
of exotic carpets. I imagined the splendour and richness of
glowing colours and exuberant patterns and that mental image
inspired this design.

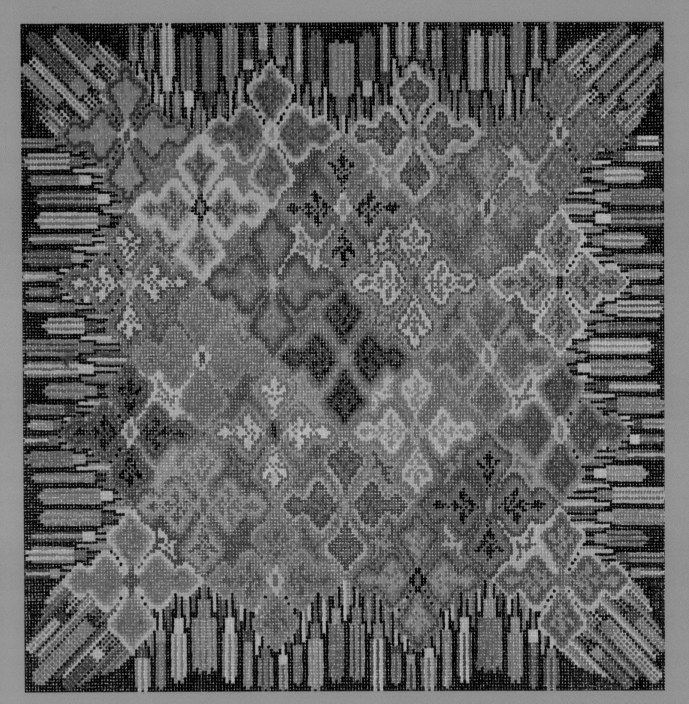

Painted artwork for 'Kasbah'
The inspiration for this design came from a captivating image from the same collection of old sepia photographs, of a camel bedecked in glorious fabrics and copious bundles of hanging tassels.

Paisleys

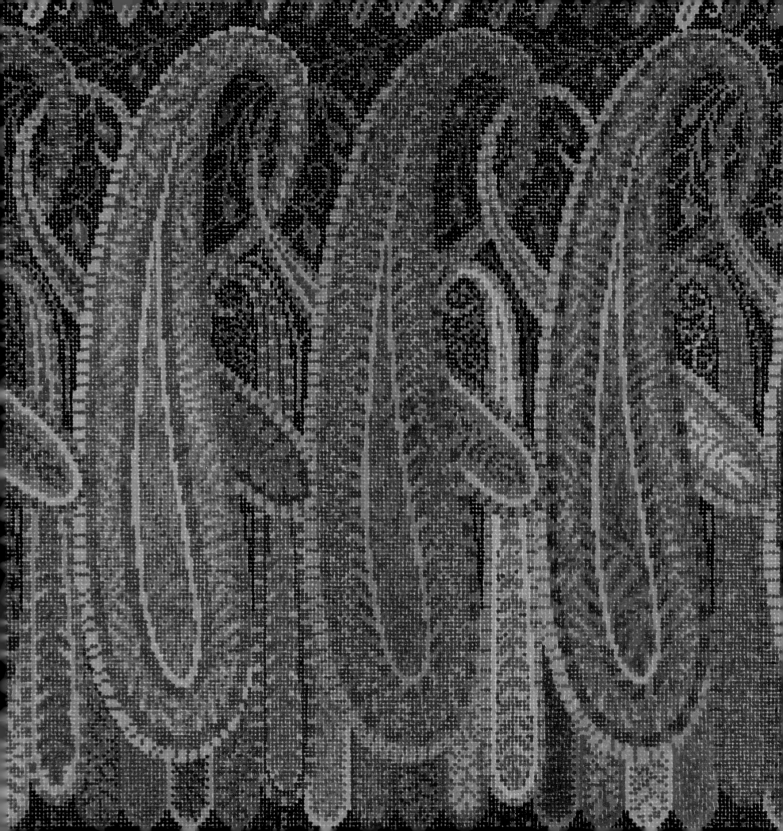

Painted artwork for 'Punjabi Paisley'
Over the years I have created many Paisley designs for printed textiles. I relish designing a new Paisley. I love the intrinsic sinuous quality of a Paisley shape and enjoy stretching and twisting the proportions to create a variety of flowing pattern which I can adorn with lavish decoration.

Painted artwork for 'Summer Paisley'
I began designing this Paisley by drawing some small, pretty flowers
which I had picked whilst having a leisurely walk along a country
lane one summer's evening, hence the name

Painted artwork for 'Indian Garden'
Reading exotic tales about the mystique of India
aroused my imagination to create this design.

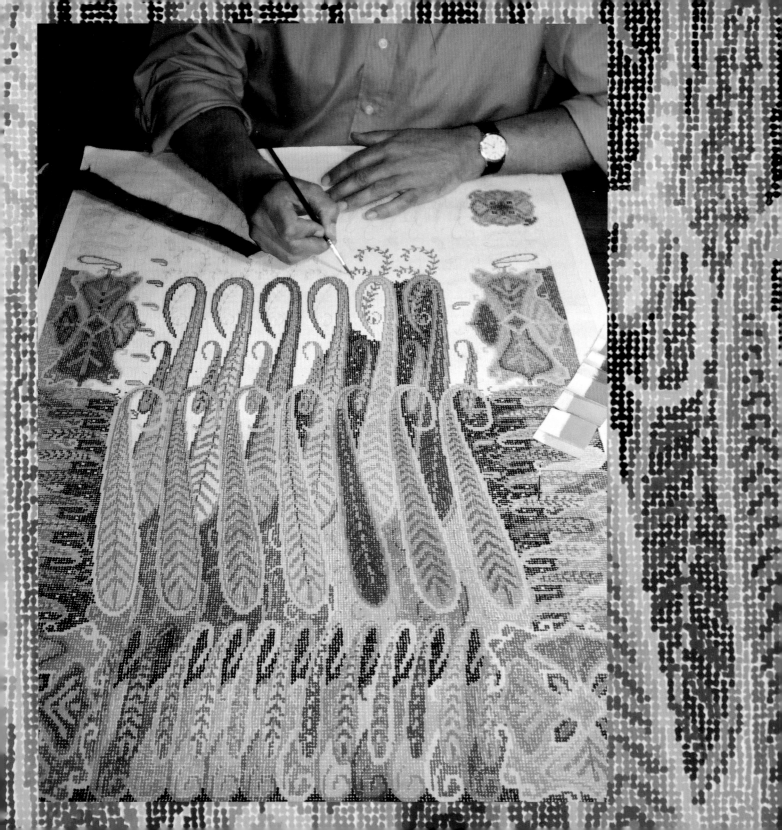

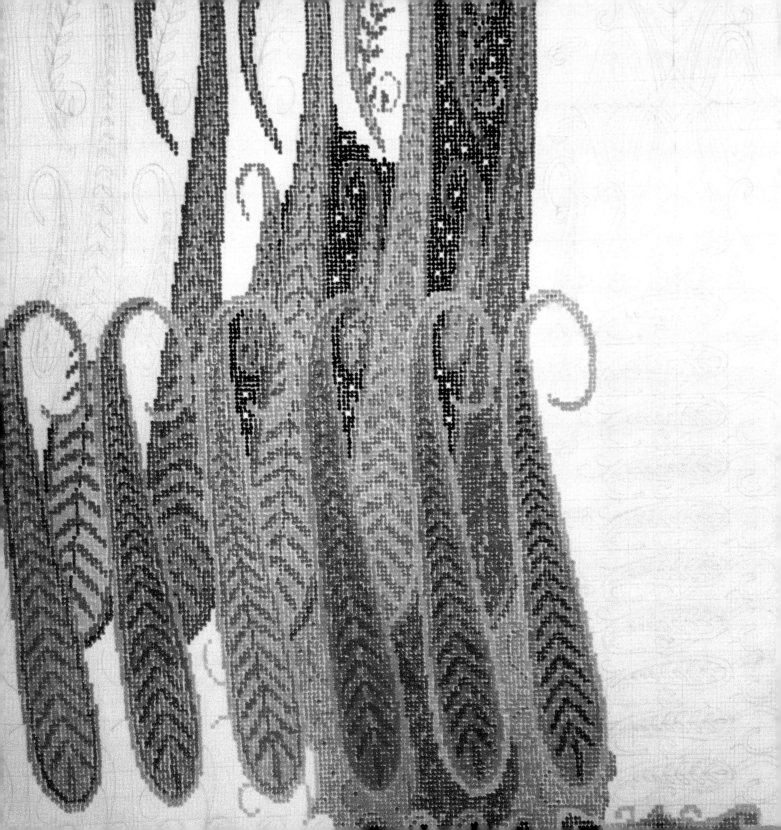

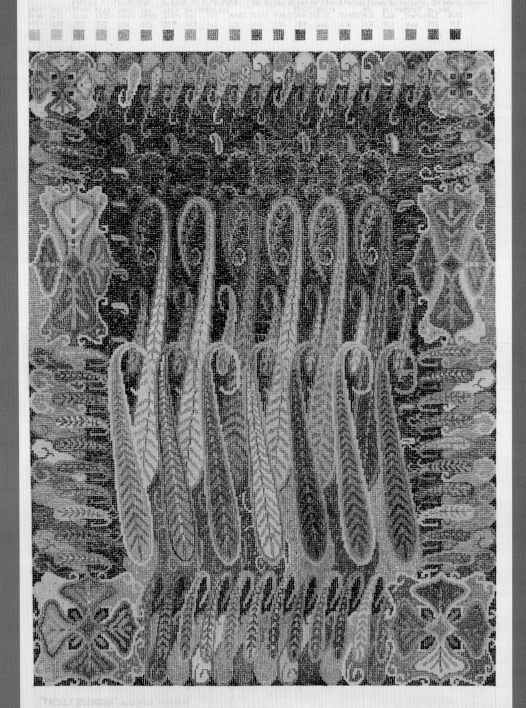

Painted artwork for 'Paisley Splendour'
This design was produced as a limited edition.
I love highly decorative flowing pattern and
for this design I created several different bands
of repeating Paisley motifs which I then
combined merging one pattern into another. The
inspiration for the colours came from bunches of
summer flowers picked from my garden. I love
the entire process of drawing and painting my
designs, seeing them develop from drawn pencil
work through to glorious painted colour.

Fans

Painted artwork for 'Daisy Fan'
I adore fans and thought that I would like to design a cushion with a fan shape. I wanted to paint big bold flowers with luscious colours to make a glorious decorative curve and chose to draw large daisies from my garden. I was ecstatically happy with the end result and still love it.

'DAISY FAN' by RANVLND HONEDAHN

Painted artwork for 'Tartan Fan'

On a visit to the Museum of Scotland in Edinburgh I saw a display
of old traditional Scottish costume where there was a profusion of
tartans. I loved the richness of seeing one tartan against another.
On my return home I unpacked one of my old leather cases which
I knew was crammed full of tartan bits and pieces I had collected
including a piper's plaid and a couple of old kilts. There was also
a somewhat tattered Scottish lace jabot. I immediately decided to
combine different tartans and lace to create this design.

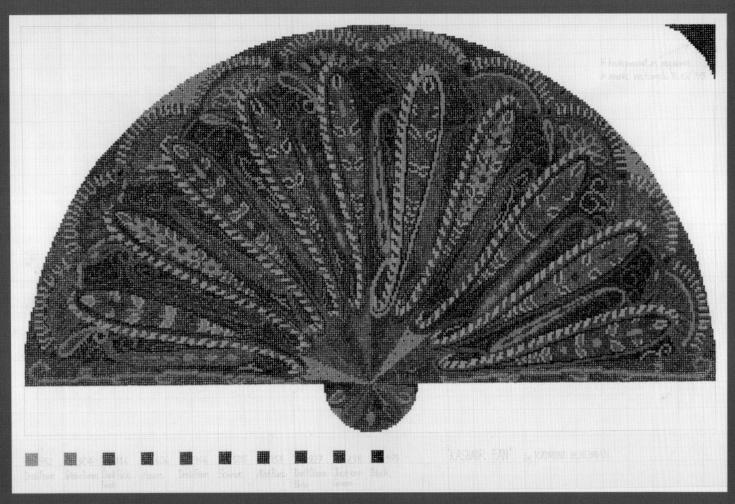

Painted artwork for 'Kashmiri Fan'
I celebrated my fondness of old Kashmir shawls and vintage
fans by creating this fan-shaped design adorned with intricate,
highly decorative motifs radiating from the centre.

Orientals

**Painted artwork for
'Mikado Maids'**
The inspiration for this design
came from seeing a film called
'Topsy-Turvy' about Gilbert
and Sullivan devising and
composing 'The Mikado'. The
magnificence of the sumptuous
colour and elaborateness of the
costumes and sets thrilled me.

Painted artwork for 'China Doll'
Designing allows me to indulge in fantasy.
I designed 'China Doll' thinking of her as a
dancer and the background as a stage set into
which she fitted perfectly, creating a vision of
shimmering colour and opulent pattern.

Painted artwork for 'Paper Fans'
A simple torn and battered paper fan bought at a second-hand market was the inspiration for this design. I love repeating the same image again and again in different colours. Although designed as a cushion I can imagine it as a resplendent wallpaper design.

Painted artwork for 'Shanghai'
This design was inspired by a visit to a breathtaking exhibition of dazzlingly colourful Chinese costumes ornately embellished with gleaming, silken embroidery.

Designed for a circular cushion
but alternative square option to
fill square with 'SKY BLUE 565'

'SHANGHAI CHRYSANTHEMUMS'
by RAYMOND HONEYMAN

BLACK 993	TURQUOISE 529	TURQUOISE 527	ROYAL BLUE 822	HYACINTH 895	CORAL 866	EARLY ENGL. GREEN 545	SKY BLUE 565	GRASS GREEN 254	FLAMINGO 626	BRIGHT MARINE 452	HYACINTH 894	EARLY ENGL. GREEN 544	BROWN 311	OLIVE DRAB GREEN 331

Florals

I love the Arts and Crafts period and would have enjoyed being a designer at that time. I created a set of designs reminiscent of the style of that era from my drawings and sketches of flowers, developing each design using sinuous line to create a gentle flow of pattern.

Painted artwork for 'Snowdrops'

Painted artwork for 'Bluebells'

Painted artwork for 'Lily of the Valley'

Painted artwork for 'Thistles'

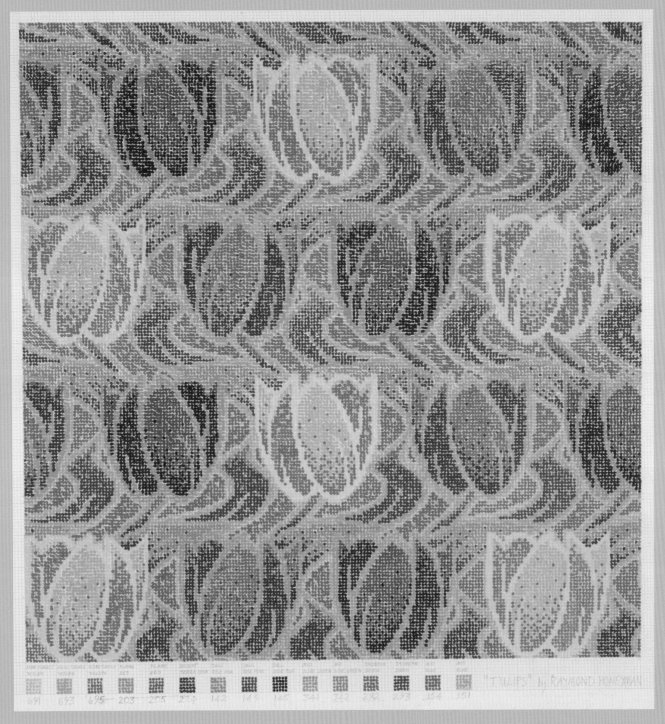

"TULIPS" by RAYMOND HONEYMAN

| HONEYSUCKLE YELLOW | JADE SHADE YELLOW | JADE SHADE YELLOW | FLAME RET | FLAME RED | BRIGHT ROSE & PINK | DEEP ROSE PINK | DEEP ROSE PINK | DEEP ROSE PINK | BLUE GREEN GREEN | BLUE GREEN GREEN | EVERGREEN GREEN | EVERGREEN GREEN | BLUE ROSE | BLUE BONE |
| 691 | 693 | 695 | 203 | 205 | 224 | 142 | 144 | 145 | 341 | 342 | 292 | 293 | 154 | 151 |

Painted artwork for 'Tulips'

'ROSES' by RAYMOND HONEYMAN

Painted artwork for 'Austrian Roses'

Painted artwork for 'Burgundy Bouquet'
The original name for this design was 'Bordeaux Bouquet' as I
sketched the idea for it whilst on holiday in Bordeaux in France.
The inspiration was seeing exquisite carved decoration on stylish
buildings of the 1930s. The change from 'Bordeaux' on the artwork
to 'Burgundy' in production remains a mystery to me.

Painted artwork for 'Bruxelles Bouquet'
I named this design after a visit to enchanting
Brussels but gave it the French spelling.

Painted artwork for 'Fleurs'

I love the charm of traditional French cafés and bars and the fact that the French cherish the faded beauty and character of old original features. It gladdens my heart that so many remain unchanged. I designed 'Fleurs' after a Christmas visit to Paris where I spent some happy hours absorbing the scintillating ambience of many cafés and bars . . . and sipping a few glasses of vin chaud. I designed it imagining it was the year 1900 and that I was designing a panel for a Parisian café. I love to fantasize.

Painted artwork for 'Persian Posy'
I began this design from the memory of having seen
an exquisite little posy bowl in an antique market.

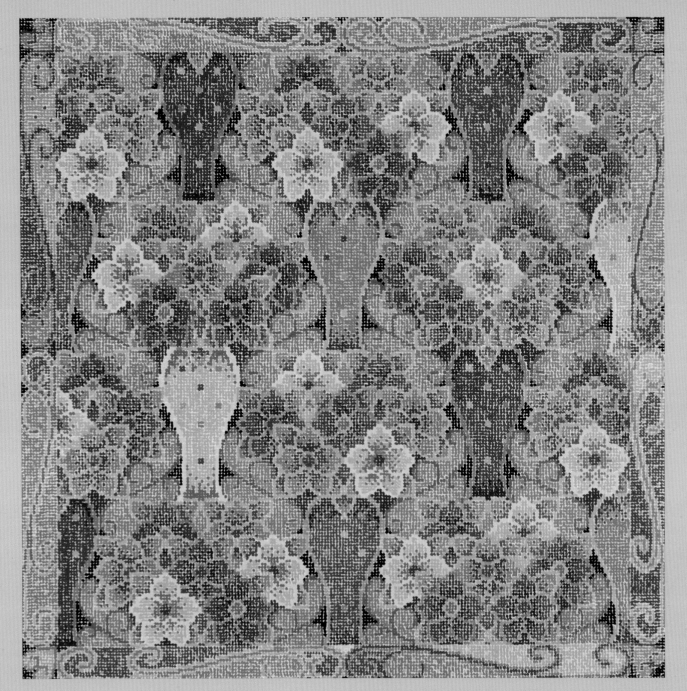

Painted artwork for 'French Flowers'
I adore Paris and my favourite area is Saint-Germain-des-Prés
on the left bank. One spring day I was passing a florist's shop
which had a bounteous array of multi-coloured bunches of
flowers displayed in the doorway. The mix of colour in the floral
bunches was stunning and I did the initial sketch for this design
that very evening.

"Designing for me is a solitary indulgence where I can create colourful, imaginative, visual fantasies."

Silk Scarves

As well as designing for the Ehrman
Tapestry collections I am delighted also to
be designing prints for the Ehrman range
of silk scarves.

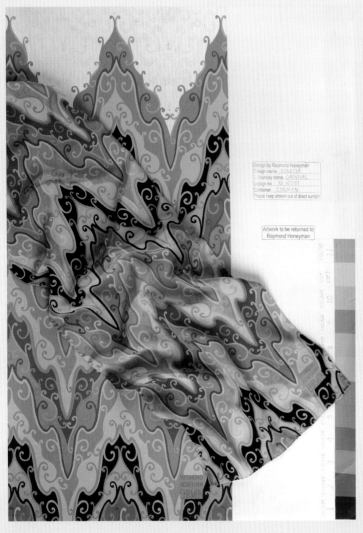

'Venezia'

This design was inspired by the architectural grandeur of Venice. The brighter colourway 'Carnival' reflects the gaiety of the carnival and the darker colourway 'Opera' suggests the glowing lights of an operatic evening in the Teatro La Fenice.

'Parisian stripe'

My idea for this scarf came on a warm lazy evening in Paris whilst strolling over the Pont Des Arts gazing at the shimmering River Seine.

I have designed this in six colourways, each after a different flower—'Rose', 'Bluebell', 'Narcissus', 'Marigold', 'Heather' and 'Poppy' (shown).